GW00468401

GRILLED

CONTENTS

INTRODUCTION

When I was young, sometimes in the summer we used to drive down to Myrtle Beach, South Carolina. Among all the good memories that I kept from those trips, I believe the best times I had were pit stops at Ponderosa Steakhouse for dinner. To be honest, the make-it-yourself ice cream sundae machines probably appealed to me more than the one-pound T-Bone steak at that age, but yet something from this place must have stayed with me. I remember quite clearly walking toward the restaurant in flip-flops, holding my parents' hands, while a gentle breeze wafted the smell of char-grilled beef and baked potatoes toward us as we approached.

I believe that mundane childhood memories like this can sometimes evolve into unexpected passions later in life, as evidenced by my passion for cooking on the grill. Whether you also have fond steakhouse memories, or simply experience everyday cravings to grill, this book is for you.

Jean-François

GRILLING WITH CHARCOAL

Explained here are all of the charcoal grilling methods we use throughout this book. This does not cover every possible grilling method, but these will give you a basic knowledge that should be enough to cook pretty much anything on a charcoal grill.

Indirect

This is referred as "indirect grilling". Place the food over the coal-free area and close the lid. This is similar to cooking in an oven but with the extra flavors that charcoal grilling brings. With this method you should be able to get your grill anywhere from 275°F up to 425°F.

Indirect with a Water Pan

Use this method for long cooking/smoking times (4+ Hours) that require low temperatures of between 200°F and 250°F. The water evaporation will damp the coals, preventing them from burning too hot. It will also contribute to keeping your meat moist during the smoking process

Two-Zone

Use this method when you want to use both "direct" and "indirect" grilling areas. Especially useful when grilling meats like chicken, for example, where you want some extra grill marks but can't leave the meat over direct heat the whole time.

Medium Heat

This method is especially useful for grilling burgers, hot dogs, and seafood. The thin bed of hot coals will give you just what you need so you can have your burgers cooked to perfection without burning them on the surface.

Minion Method

This method consists of placing a small amount of lit coals onto a large amount of unlit charcoal. When doing this, the charcoal will slowly light its way down and provide a consistent heat during several hours. Mostly used for smokers, this technique can also be made in regular charcoal kettle grills.

High Heat

Use this method to achieve maximum heat when a good sear is required. You'll notice the coal-free area on the first quarter of the grill; when working with that much heat, you always want to keep a safety zone in the event that things get out of control.

SIDES
& APPETIZERS

JALAPENO CHEESEBURGER POPPERS

Recommended for
Charcoal or gas grill

Cooking time
20 min to 30 min

Serves
4 to 6

Ground beef in a spicy jalapeño boat, topped with melted cheese and a slice of crispy bacon will not only smell divine while cooking but will also count as one of the vegetables in your five-a-day. Mix some of the seeds back in for an extra kick.

1 Preheat your grill for indirect;

2 Mix the ground beef, cream cheese, worcestershire sauce and black pepper;

3 Cut each jalapeño in half lengthwise and core the interior. Fill each half jalapeño with the ground beef mixture then top with a slice of cheddar cheese and wrap with half a slice of bacon;

4 Thread poppers onto skewers;

5 Toss a handful of wood chips onto hot coals (preferably hickory and/or apple) and cook in indirect for 20 minutes or until the bacon is done.

Poppers
6 jalapeño peppers
½ pound ground beef, cooked
⅓ cup cream cheese
1 Tbsp worcestershire sauce
6 slices of bacon, halfway cooked
12 slices of cheddar cheese
1 tsp ground black pepper

Additional Equipment
1 cup hickory and/or apple wood chips
skewers

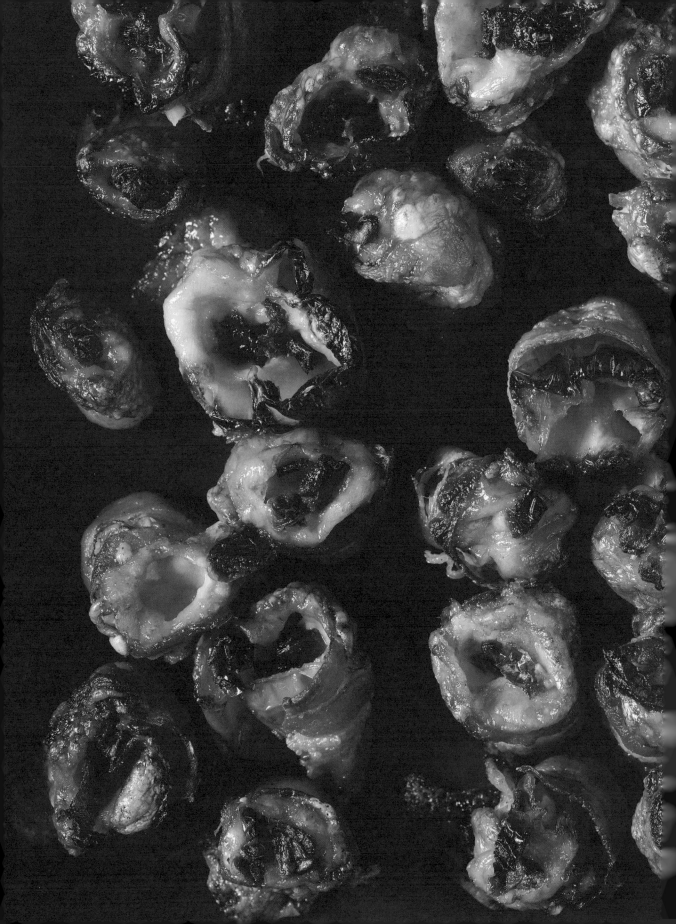

HABANERO
POPPERS

Poppers

24 habanero peppers

2 ½ cup aged cheddar cheese, shredded

12 slices of bacon

1 cup sun-dried tomatoes, minced

wood chunks, preferably pecan and/or hickory

Additional Equipment

skewers

HABANERO POPPERS

Recommended for	Cooking time	Serves
Smoker	1h 30 to 2 h	4 to 6

These super-hot cheesy stuffed habaneros will add excitement to any occasion. Cool it down with creme fraiche or your favorite dipping sauce.

1 Preheat your smoker at 250°F;

2 With a knife, core each habanero to remove the interior; Fill each one with shredded aged cheddar cheese then wrap them in bacon; Place a teaspoon of minced sun-dried tomatoes on top;

3 Thread the poppers onto skewers to prevent them from falling on their side while cooking;

4 Smoke for 1h30 to 2 hours at 250°F, or until the bacon is fully cooked;

Serve with sour cream or your favorite dipping sauce.

JAMAICAN JERK CHICKEN WINGS

Recommended for	Cooking time	Serves
Charcoal or gas grill	30 min to 45 min	3 to 6

Scotch bonnet hot sauce mixed with highly fragrant spices will give these chicken wings some depth and flavor like you've never seen. These West Indies hot wings will soon become a firm favorite with friends and family.

1 Mix all ingredients but the chicken wings together to form a wet rub; Apply the rub on the wings and let marinate for 2 to 4 hours in the refrigerator;

2 Preheat your grill for a two-zone cooking, having hot coals on one end and nothing on the other;

3 Sear the chicken wings over high heat for 3 to 4 minutes per side then move to indirect and close the lid;
Cooking time: 30 to 45 minutes at 350°F; Serve and enjoy.

Wings
20 chicken wings
2 Tbsp scotch bonnet or habanero hot sauce
⅓ cup cane sugar
¼ cup scallions, chopped
1 garlic clove, minced
1 ½ Tbsp dried thyme
1 Tbsp paprika
1 Tbsp allspice
1 Tbsp ground ginger
1 Tbsp salt
½ Tbsp ground black pepper
1 tsp ground cinnamon
½ tsp ground nutmeg
¼ cup olive oil
juice from 1 lime

NACHO WINGS

Recommended for	Cooking time	Serves
Charcoal or gas grill	20 min to 30 min	4 to 6

In typical nacho style, these wings are topped with a double cheese blend along with tangy pickled peppers, barbecue sauce and crumbled bacon. Try adding a cool ranch or creamy blue cheese dip for enhancing the fun.

1 Preheat your grill for medium heat;

2 Brush the wings with canola oil then season with paprika, brown sugar, cayenne powder, salt and pepper;

3 Grill the wings over direct heat for about 8 to 12 minutes per side with the lid closed; Rotate and move the wings frequently if needed to prevent them from burning;

4 Place the grilled chicken wings vertically in a cast iron skillet with the meatier section on top — to do this, start by placing the wings next to an edge of the skillet and fill the entire pan until they have no space to move;

5 Cover with all topping ingredients and place back into the grill for 8 to 10 more minutes; Serve with a ranch or blue cheese dip (optional) and enjoy.

Wings
12 pounds chicken wings
2 Tbsp canola oil
2 Tbsp paprika
2 Tbsp brown sugar
½ Tbsp cayenne powder
½ Tbsp salt
½ Tbsp black pepper

Toppings
⅔ cup cheddar cheese, shredded
⅔ cup monterey jack cheese, shredded
⅔ cup mozzarella cheese, shredded
½ cup crumbled bacon
¼ cup red onions, chopped
¼ cup pickled hot peppers
2 Tbsp bbq sauce
juice from half a lime

Additional Equipment
½ cup wood chips for smoking (optional)

BUFFALO CHICKEN WINGS

Recommended for
Charcoal or gas grill

Cooking time
30 min to 45 min

Serves
3 to 6

Inspired by a classic, we traded some of the heat for an extra layer of flavor in this tomato-based variation. These party favorites will keep people coming back for more.

1 Preheat your grill for indirect;

2 In a bowl, mix the wings with olive oil and lemon juice then season with salt and pepper;

3 Cook for 20 minutes in indirect at about 450°F;

4 In a preheated cast iron skillet, mix all Buffalo Sauce ingredients and bring to a simmer for 10 minutes;

5 Submerge the wings into the buffalo sauce, then place them back on the grill and sear for 2 to 3 minutes over high heat. Serve with your favorite ranch or blue cheese dip (optional); Enjoy.

Wings
20 chicken wings
2 Tbsp olive oil
½ Tbsp salt
½ Tbsp black pepper
1 Tbsp lemon juice

Buffalo Sauce
½ cup melted butter
½ cup cayenne hot sauce
⅔ cup tomato sauce
1 ½ Tbsp chili powder
1 tsp cayenne pepper flakes

BOLD & SMOKY WINGS

Recommended for	Cooking time	Serves
Charcoal or gas grill	45 min to 1 h	4 to 6

Sweet and spicy barbecue at its best. Cooked in indirect at 400°F, this recipe calls for the crispiest skin you'll ever get from smoked chicken wings.

1 Preheat your grill for indirect at 400°F;

2 Mix the cayenne powder, onion powder, brown sugar, paprika, salt and pepper in a bowl; Brush the chicken wings with canola oil and season with the rub;

3 Place the wings on the grill for indirect; Toss a few wood chunks onto hot coals and close the lid; Cook 35 to 45 minutes at 400°F;

4 Prepare the Sweet & Spicy BBQ Sauce while the wings are cooking; Mix all ingredients in a saucepan and simmer for 10 minutes;

5 Brush the wings with the Sweet & Spicy BBQ Sauce for the last 5 to 10 minutes of cooking;

6 Remove from the grill and serve with the remaining BBQ Sauce on the side.

Chicken Wings
20 to 30 chicken wings
3 Tbsp canola oil
2 tsp cayenne powder
2 tsp onion powder
1 Tbsp brown sugar
1 tsp paprika
2 tsp salt
1 tsp ground black pepper

Sweet & Spicy BBQ Sauce
16 oz ketchup
½ cup brown sugar
½ cup apple cider vinegar
¼ cup apple juice
¼ cup honey
½ Tbsp worcestershire sauce
½ tsp salt
½ tsp ground black pepper
¼ tsp ground celery seeds
½ Tbsp red pepper flakes
1½ Tbsp jalapeño hot sauce

Additional Equipment
2 to 3 woods chunks for smoking, preferably apple and hickory

**ROOT BEER
CHICKEN WINGS**

Wings

40 chicken wings
¼ cup olive oil
½ Tbsp grated ginger
½ Tbsp grated orange zest
1 Tbsp salt
1 Tbsp ground black pepper
½ tsp vanilla extract
juice from one orange

Root Beer BBQ Sauce

1 cup root beer
1 cup ketchup
3 Tbsp worcestershire sauce
3 Tbsp brown sugar
½ tsp onion powder
½ tsp garlic powder
1 tsp salt
1 tsp ground black pepper
juice from half a lemon

ROOT BEER CHICKEN WINGS

Recommended for	Cooking time	Serves
Charcoal or gas grill	25 min to 30 min	6 to 10

The aromas of spices and vanilla that you will achieve when grilling these chicken wings are priceless. Combined with a slightly caramelized root beer barbecue sauce, this delightful dish will make your guests feel in good hands.

1 Preheat your grill for a two-zone cooking — having hot coals on one side and nothing on the other; If you are using a gas grill, turn half the burners to high and leave the other half closed;

2 Mix the olive oil, grated ginger, orange zest, orange juice, vanilla extract, 1 Tbsp of salt and 1 Tbsp of black pepper with the chicken wings and let marinate for 30 minutes in the refrigerator;

3 Grill the wings over high heat for 3 to 4 minutes per side, then move to indirect; Close the lid and cook for 20 to 25 minutes at 450°F;

4 In a cast iron skillet, combine all Root Beer BBQ Sauce ingredients and bring to a simmer for 10 minutes;

5 Brush the wings with the Root Beer BBQ Sauce then place them over high heat one last time for the sauce to caramelize, about 1 to 2 minutes; Serve with orange slices and a cold rich-tasting root beer (optional); Enjoy.

CHILI LIME JERKY

Recommended for	Cooking time	Serves
Smoker	4 h to 6 h	6 to 10

Long days spent smoking massive quantities of beef jerky became a tradition for us. We would put the beef to marinate the night before and fire up the smoker early in the morning. This chili lime jerky makes the best snack for road trips and outdoor activities of any sort.

1 In a bowl, make the marinade by mixing all ingredients except the beef;

2 Cut the beef roast into thin slices of 1/8 to 1/4 inches thick (you can leave the roast for 15 minutes in the freezer beforehand to make it easier to slice); Place the slices of beef into the marinade and store in the refrigerator for 4 to 6 hours;

3 Preheat your smoker at 200 to 225°F;

4 Remove the beef slices from the marinade – If you want to maximize space in your smoker, thread each beef slices onto skewers and have them hang vertically from your smoker's grill grate (see preparation pictures);

5 Toss 5 or 6 wood chunks onto hot coals and smoke the beef jerky for 4 to 6 hours or until desired texture.

Jerky
4 lb beef round (any cuts)
2 Tbsp chili powder
1 Tbsp ancho chili
1 Tbsp ground cayenne
1 Tbsp onion powder
1 Tbsp garlic powder
1 Tbsp black pepper
½ cup honey
2 Tbsp worcestershire sauce
½ cup soy sauce
juice and zest from 2 limes

Additional Equipment
wood chunks for smoking, preferably a blend of hickory, apple and/or cherry
skewers (optional)

BEER-CANDIED BACON

Recommended for
Charcoal or gas grill

Cooking time
30 min to 45 min

Serves
4 to 6

Candied Bacon
1 to 2 pounds hardwood smoked bacon
2 ¼ cups brown sugar
1 cup brown ale beer

Additional Equipment
basting brush

Hardwood smoked bacon strips drenched in brown ale and coated with brown sugar. These sweet and tasty beer-candied snacks will be a hit with family and friends, so remember to cook plenty.

1 Preheat your grill for indirect;

2 Mix 2 cups of brown sugar with 1 cup of beer and whisk until the sugar has fully dissolved; Brush the bacon on both side with the beer syrup and sprinkle some more brown sugar on top;

3 Cook the bacon in indirect for 30 to 45 minutes at about 350°F; Frequently flip the slices and brush with some extra beer syrup; Repeat 4 to 6 times until the bacon is fully cooked (don't worry if the slices still seem soft by then, they will harden upon cooling);

4 Let cool at room temperature for 20 minutes before serving.

ARMADILLO
EGGS

Armadillo Eggs

12 jalapeños

1 cup cream cheese

1 cup cheddar cheese, shredded

2 ½ lb sausage meat

Additional Equipment

wood chunks for smoking, preferably hickory and/or pecan

ARMADILLO EGGS

Recommended for	Cooking time	Serves
Smoker	1 h 30 to 2 h	4 to 6

If you and your friends can handle a little heat then these tasty bite-sized nibbles are perfect for your next get-together. Creamy on the inside and crisp on the outside, leave in some extra seeds for an additional kick.

1 Preheat your smoker at 250°F; To make this recipe in a regular charcoal grill, place a small amount of hot coals next to an aluminum foil pan filled with water and adjust the air vent on the lid so that the holes are almost closed;

2 Cut off the top from each jalapeño and remove the interior using a jalapeño corer tool or a vegetable peeler;

3 Mix the two cheeses together, then stuff the filling inside each emptied jalapeño; Separate the sausage meat into 12 equal patties then wrap each one around a stuffed jalapeño; Make sure the peppers are fully wrapped and not visible;

4 Place the armadillo eggs in the smoker and toss a handful of wood chunks onto hot coals; Cook for 1h30 to 2h at 250°F.

PULLED PORK POTATO SKINS

Recommended for
Charcoal or gas grill

Cooking time
20 min

Serves
4 to 8

Potato Skins
4 russet potatoes, fully cooked
3 cups leftover pulled pork
¾ cup bbq sauce
1 cup shredded cheddar cheese
¼ cup red onions, minced
coleslaw (optional)

These stuffed potato skins are the perfect addition to any meal and a great way to use up leftover pulled pork.

1 Preheat your grill of indirect;

2 Cut the baked potatoes in half lengthwise and empty the inside with a spoon; Mix the pulled pork and bbq sauce together then fill in each potato skin; Top with shredded cheese;

3 Cook in indirect for 15 to 20 minutes;

4 Top with red onions and/or coleslaw (optional) and serve.

CEDAR PLANKED BRIE

Recommended for
Charcoal or gas grill

Cooking time
20 min

Serves
4 to 8

The aromas of sizzling cedar mixed with fruits, grilled almonds, and fresh herbs will take any regular brie wheel to another level.

1 Preheat your grill at 400°F;

2 Mix the strawberry jam and white wine in a bowl then divide into two equal portions; Add the raspberries to one portion and the blackberries to the other;

3 Place both brie wheels on the pre-soaked cedar plank; Rub with brown sugar, pour the fruit/wine jam on top and sprinkle some freshly chopped thyme leaves; Add some almonds on the empty spaces of the plank (optional);

4 Cook with the lid closed for 20 to 25 min at 400°F; Serve with french baguette.

Brie
2 wheels of brie cheese, 8 to 12 oz each
⅔ cup strawberry jam
⅓ cup fresh raspberries
⅓ cup fresh blackberries
¼ cup dry white wine
2 Tbsp brown sugar
½ Tbsp chopped fresh thyme
almonds (optional)

Additional Equipment
cedar plank, soaked in water for 2 hours

BURGERS

DOGS AND SANDWICHES

LONG BOY BURGERS

Recommended for
Charcoal or gas grill

Cooking time
6 min to 10 min

Serves
4 to 6

Grilled cheesy meat loaf on a bun, finished with a layer of crumbled bacon and freshly chopped chives. This is comfort food like you've never seen before.

1 Preheat your grill for direct grilling over medium heat;

2 Mix all the ingredients except the chives, cheese, bacon and bread in a bowl; Divide into 4 to 6 equal patties and shape them in the form of your sub rolls;

3 Grill for 3 to 4 minutes over direct heat then flip and add the shredded cheddar cheese and crumbled bacon on top; Close the lid and cook for another 3 to 4 minutes;

4 Serve on sub rolls and top with freshly chopped chives.

Burgers
1 ½ lb ground beef
¼ cup corn flakes, crushed
¼ cup crispy fried onions
1 tsp dried thyme
1 tsp garlic powder
1 egg
2 Tbsp ketchup
1 Tbsp worcestershire sauce
3 Tbsp milk
1 cup shredded cheddar cheese
2 Tbsp chives, chopped
½ cup crumbled bacon
4 to 6 sub rolls

TEQUILA BURGERS WITH CHIPOTLE MAYO

Recommended for
Charcoal or gas grill

Cooking time
30 min to 45 min

Serves
6

Bet you never thought of combining tequila in grilled prime beef burgers. This recipe's got you covered: honey roasted potatoes, chipotle mayo, and one of the most memorable burgers you'll ever have.

1 Preheat your grill for a two-zone cooking — having hot coals on one end and nothing on the other; If you are using a gas grill, turn half of the burners to high and leave the other half closed;

2 In a cast iron skillet, mix all Honey Roasted Potatoes ingredients and cook in indirect for 25 to 35 minutes at 400°F;

3 Combine the egg yolk, dijon mustard and the ice cube in a food processor and start to blend; Very slowly pour the canola and olive oil mix while the food processor is running — You should stretch the pouring time to about 1 minute; Finally add the remaining Chipotle Mayo ingredients and continue to blend for another 20 to 30 sec;

4 In a bowl, mix the ground beef, tequila, shredded cheddar cheese, salt and pepper, then form 6 equal burger patties;

5 Grill the burgers over direct heat for about 3 to 6 minutes per side, or until desired doneness;

6 Assemble with grilled burger buns, chipotle mayo, and your favorite choice of condiments.

Burgers
2 ½ pounds ground beef
6 oz tequila
1 cup shredded cheddar cheese
6 slices of American cheese
6 burger buns
tomatoes, lettuce & red onions and your favorite condiments

Chipotle Mayo
1 egg yolk
1 Tbsp dijon mustard
1 ice cube
½ cup canola oil
½ cup olive oil
1 tsp salt
1 tsp black pepper
1 Tbsp cider vinegar
1 chipotle pepper in adobo sauce
juice from half a lime

Honey Roasted Potatoes
6 russet potatoes, sliced into thick cut fries
⅓ cup vegetable oil
2 Tbsp honey
2 garlic cloves, minced
½ Tbsp dried oregano
½ Tbsp salt
½ Tbsp black pepper
juice from half a lime

Additional Equipment
food processor

LUTHER BURGER

Recommended for
Charcoal or gas grill

Cooking time
8 min to 10 min

Serves
4

Also called doughnut burgers, this American-style burger will tantalize your taste buds and liven up the party.

1 Preheat your grill for a two-zone cooking: set one side to medium/high and the other to low temperature;

2 Mix the ground beef with the worcestershire sauce and fried onions then form 4 equal patties; Add salt and pepper to taste;

3 Place the bacon slices over low heat and close the lid 6 to 10 minutes; Keep an eye on the grill in case there are flare ups;

4 Flip the bacon and then place the burgers over medium/high for 3 to 4 minutes per side; Add a slice of American cheese on top of each burger a minute before they are done;

5 Grill each donut for 5 to 10 seconds per side;

6 Assemble the burgers with two grilled donuts and a slice of bacon.

Burgers
1 ½ lb ground beef
4 slices of bacon
4 slices of American cheese
8 glazed donuts
2 Tbsp worcestershire sauce
¼ cup fried onions
salt and black pepper to taste

SURF 'N' TURF BURGERS

Recommended for	**Cooking time**	**Serves**
Charcoal or gas grill	6 min to 10 min	4 to 5

Nothing beats quality home-grilled sirloin beef burgers, especially when you team it with a slice of Swiss cheese and some serious jumbo shrimp.

1 Preheat your grill for direct grilling over medium heat;

2 Mix the Aïoli Mayo ingredients in a bowl and set aside in the refrigerator;

3 With a sharp Chef's Knife, cut the beef sirloin into thin slabs, slice the slabs into thin spaghetti like strips then turn 90 degrees and cut into 1/8 to 1/4 long pieces — or use a meat grinder if you have one;

4 Mix the ground sirloin with 2 Tbsp of barbecue rub, 1 Tbsp of breadcrumbs and 1 egg; Form 4 to 5 equal patties of about 1 inch thick;

5 Thread the shrimp onto flat skewers and season both sides with barbecue rub;

6 Place the shrimp and burgers on your hot grill grate and cook for 3 to 4 minutes per side; Place a slice of Swiss cheese on top of each burgers for the last 30 seconds; You can let the burgers cook a little longer if you prefer them well done;

7 Assemble the burgers in toasted buns with a spoonful of aïoli mayo, some rocket salad and three grilled shrimp; Serve and enjoy.

Burgers
2 lb beef sirloin
¼ cup all-purpose barbecue rub
1 Tbsp breadcrumbs
1 egg
4 slices of Swiss cheese
12 jumbo shrimp (8-12)
1 cup rocket salad
burger buns

Aïoli Mayo
⅔ cup mayonnaise
1 Tbsp whole grain mustard
1 clove garlic, crushed
1 tsp oregano
½ tsp salt
the juice from half a lemon

Additional Equipment
skewers
meat grinder (optional)

CHILI CHEESE
DOGS

Hot Dogs

6 all beef jumbo-sized
hot dogs
6 hot dog buns
1 cup shredded cheddar
cheese

Chili

1 Tbsp canola oil
1 ½ cup onions, chopped
3 garlic cloves, minced
1 ½ lb ground beef
1 Tbsp chili powder
1 tsp dried oregano
1 tsp cinnamon
1 tsp unsweetened cocoa
powder
1 tsp ground cumin
½ tsp ground allspice
1 tsp salt
1 tsp black pepper
½ cup tomato sauce
3 Tbsp ketchup
1 Tbsp red wine vinegar
1 Tbsp worcestershire
sauce

Additional Equipment

cast iron skillet

CHILI CHEESE DOGS

Recommended for	Cooking time	Serves
Charcoal or gas grill	25 min to 30 min	6 to 8

1 Preheat your grill for a two-zone cooking — having hot coals on one side and nothing on the other; If you are using a gas grill, turn half the burners to high and leave the other half closed;

2 In preheated cast iron skillet, saute the onions and garlic with canola oil until golden brown, then add the ground beef and cook for 2 to 3 minutes;

3 Whisk in all remaining chili ingredients, then move the skillet to indirect; Close the lid and cook for 20 minutes;

4 Place the hot dogs over direct heat and grill for 2 to 4 minutes per side;

5 Assemble each hot dog with grilled buns, hot chili, and shredded cheddar cheese.

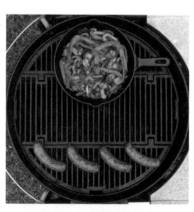

SAUSAGE & PEPPER HEROES

Recommended for	Cooking time	Serves
Charcoal or gas grill	20 min to 35 min	4

Smoked beef sausages served with crispy bacon, sautéd peppers and onions, and topped with a delicious homemade chipotle mayo.

1 Preheat your grill for a two-zone cooking — having hot coals on one side and nothing on the other; If you are using a gas grill, turn half the burners to high and leave the other half closed;

2 Combine all Chipotle Mayo ingredients in a bowl, then pour into a squeeze bottle; Keep in the fridge until ready to use;

3 Place the bacon in a cast iron skillet over direct heat and cook halfway; Add the chopped bell peppers, onions, worcestershire and black pepper; Continue to cook until the peppers are soft and lightly roasted and the bacon is fully cooked;

4 Move the skillet to indirect and place 4 sausage links over direct heat; close the lid and cook for 5 to 6 minutes per side;

5 Mix the melted butter with dried basil and brush the top of each sub roll; Assemble each sandwich with sautéed vegetables and bacon, then add the mozzarella cheese on top; Bring the heroes back to the grill for indirect cooking and close the lid for 10 minutes.

Heroes

4 links of beef sausages

¼ cup melted butter

1 tsp dried basil

4 sub rolls

1 cup mozzarella cheese, shredded

½ cup bacon, sliced

1 red bell pepper, sliced

1 green bell pepper, sliced

1 red onion, sliced

1 Tbsp worcestershire sauce

ground black pepper to taste

freshly chopped chives for topping

Chipotle Mayo

1 cup mayonnaise

¼ cup yellow mustard

2 Tbsp honey

1 Tbsp pureed chipotle in adobo sauce

juice from half a lime

ALL-IN BREAKFAST SANDWICHES

Recommended for
Charcoal or gas grill

Cooking time
20 min to 30 min

Serves
4

These applewood smoked breakfast sandwiches go above and beyond all expectations. Serve them with grilled chipotle potatoes, baked beans, and a nice cup of coffee to start your day on the right foot.

1 Preheat your grill for a two-zone cooking — having hot coals on one side and nothing on the other; If you are using a gas grill, turn half the burners to high and leave the other half closed;

2 Cut the potatoes into slices of a half inch thick and baste both sides with vegetable oil; Season with chipotle powder, oregano, salt and pepper;

3 Divide the sausage meat into 4 equal patties and shape each into a bowl; Wrap each bowl with a slice of bacon;

4 Toss a handful of wood chips onto hot coals for smoking and place the meat bowls and potatoes over indirect heat; Close the lid and cook for 25 to 30 minutes at 350°F;

5 Crack an egg into each meat bowl and cook for 10 more minutes; If you want some baked beans with breakfast, now is the time to add them to the grill - Pour a can of beans in a cast iron skillet and place over direct heat while the eggs are cooking;

6 Assemble each sandwich with grilled English muffins, grilled onions, and a slice of American cheese.

Sandwiches
1 lb sausage meat
4 slices of bacon
4 eggs
4 slices of American cheese
1 red onion
4 English muffins
freshly cracked black pepper to taste
a can of baked beans (optional)

Chipotle Smoked Breakfast Potatoes
3 to 4 russet potatoes
¼ cup vegetable oil
1 Tbsp chipotle powder
½ Tbsp dried oregano
½ Tbsp black pepper
½ Tbsp salt

Additional Equipment
wood chips for smoking, preferably apple

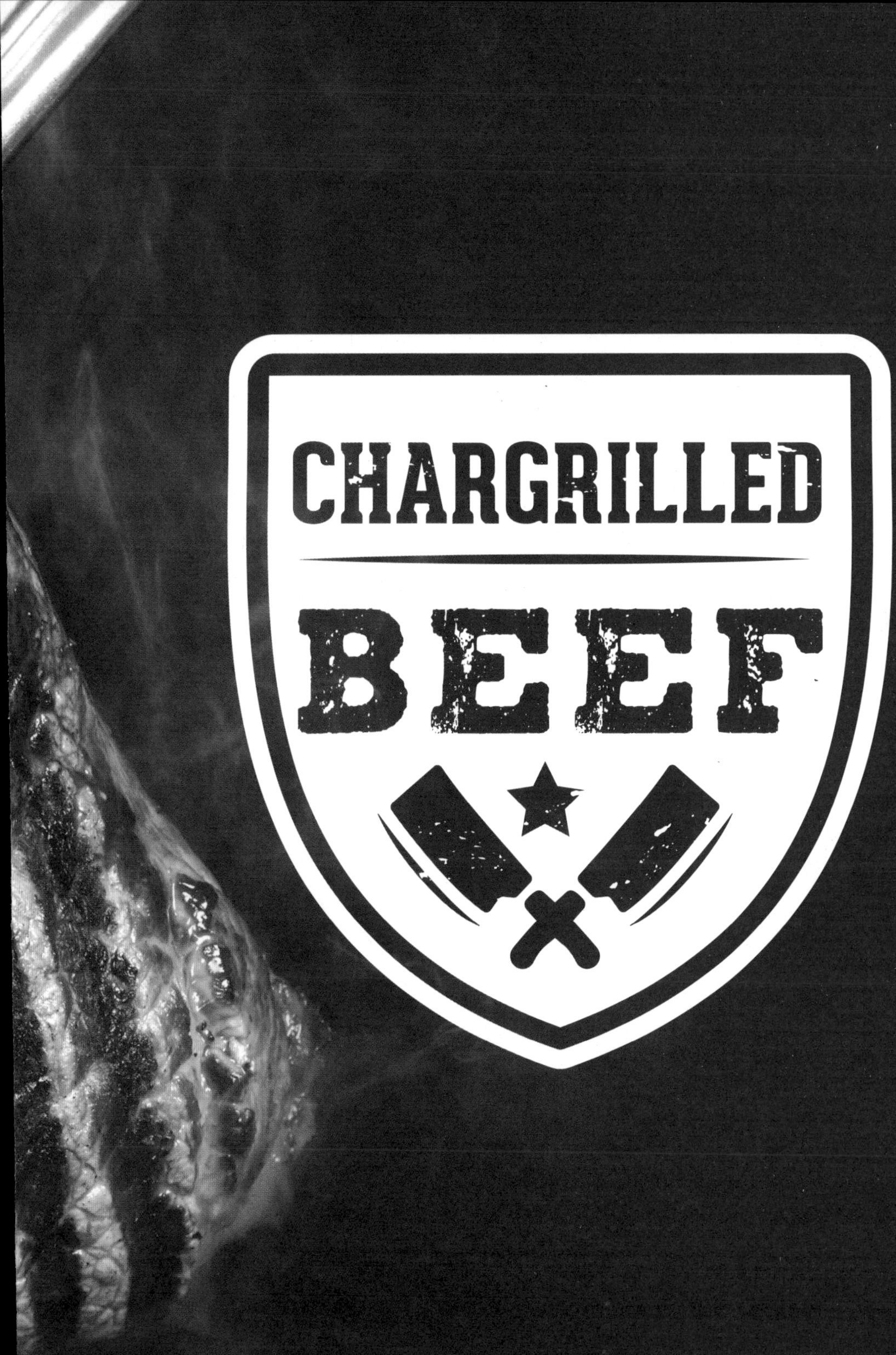
CHARGRILLED
BEEF

HICKORY PLANKED
CHEESESTEAK

Sandwiches

1 bone-in ribeye,
2 inches thick
½ Tbsp ground black pepper
½ Tbsp coarse sea salt
1 cup chopped green peppers
1 cup chopped mushrooms
1 cup chopped onions
4 slices provolone cheese
4 amoroso bread

Vinegar Sauce

1 Tbsp cayenne pepper flakes
1 Tbsp ground black pepper
1 Tbsp garlic salt
½ cup white vinegar
¼ cup olive oil
¼ cup water
1 Tbsp balsamic vinegar

Additional Equipment

hickory grilling plank, soaked in water for 30 min
squeeze bottle (optional)

HICKORY PLANKED CHEESESTEAK

Recommended for	Cooking time	Serves
Charcoal or gas grill	30 min	4

The beauty of grilling steak on a hickory wood plank is that you can literally let the plank catch fire for a few seconds and close the lid to tame down the flames and generate an additional layer of smoked flavors. This variation of a Philly Cheesesteak is a game changer.

1 Preheat your grill for indirect;

2 Combine the Vinegar Sauce ingredients in a squeeze bottle, shake and set aside;

3 Grill the ribeye steak over high heat for 2 minutes per side; Move to a butcher block and cut into slices of about ¼ inches thick; Place the slices on the hickory plank, add salt and pepper to taste and bring back to the grill; Cook over direct heat with the lid closed for 20 minutes;

4 In a preheated cast iron skillet, sauté the vegetable in olive oil for about 5 minutes then spray about ½ cup or more of the vinegar sauce over the sizzling vegetables and ribeye slices; Add the provolone cheese on top of the meat and cook for 10 more minutes;

5 Assemble the sandwiches with amoroso breads, mayonnaise, dijon mustard or your favorite choice of condiments.

Chargrilled Beef

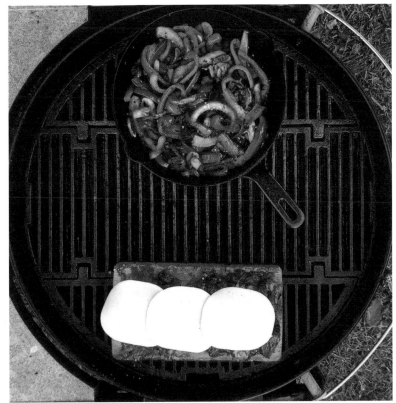

TOMAHAWK WITH CHIMICHURRI ROJO

Steak

1 tomahawk steak,
2 ½ inches thick
2 tsp coarse sea salt
2 tsp freshly cracked black pepper
1 tsp garlic powder
1 tsp chipotle flakes

Chimichurri Rojo

⅓ cup red wine vinegar
⅓ cup olive oil
¼ cup fresh parsley
2 Tbsp fresh oregano
juice from 1 lemon
1 red bell pepper
1 roma tomato
3 garlic cloves
2 Tbsp paprika
1 Tbsp cayenne flakes
1 tsp ground cumin
1 tsp salt
1 tsp black pepper

TOMAHAWK WITH CHIMICHURRI ROJO

Recommended for	Cooking time	Serves
Charcoal or gas grill	20 min to 30 min	2 to 5

1 Preheat your grill for indirect grilling;

2 Season the tomahawk steak on both sides with coarse sea salt, freshly cracked black pepper, garlic granules and chipotle flakes; Let sit at room temperature for at least 20 minutes;

3 Place the tomahawk on the grill for indirect cooking and close the lid; Cook for about 20 minutes at 350°F or until the internal temperature reaches between 105 and 110°F on an instant read thermometer;

4 Combine all Chimichurri Rojo ingredients in a food processor, blend for 20 to 30 sec and set aside;

5 When the steak has reached desired internal temperature, move over direct heat and sear for 1 to 2 minutes per side; Remove from the grill and let rest at room temperature for 10 minutes;

6 Cut the steak into ¼" thick slices and pour some chimichurri rojo on top.

Prime Rib

bone-in prime rib, 8 pounds or more

Garlic & Herbs Wet Rub

⅔ cup olive oil

1 Tbsp worcestershire sauce

4 cloves garlic

¼ onion

2 Tbsp fresh parsley

1 Tbsp fresh rosemary

½ Tbsp lemon zest, grated

1 Tbsp salt

1 ½ Tbsp black pepper

Additional Equipment

oak wood chunks

aluminum drip pan

wireless instant read thermometer (optional)

OAK SMOKED PRIME RIB

Recommended for	Cooking time	Serves
Charcoal or gas grill	2 h 30 to 4 h	6 to 8

1 Preheat your grill for indirect cooking; Place an aluminum drip pan filled with water under the grate and pour a chimney of hot coals alongside to separate the two cooking zones;

2 In a food processor, blend all Garlic & Herbs Wet Rub ingredients until you get a semi-liquid paste; Pour the wet rub over the prime rib and brush on all sides;

3 Place the prime rib for indirect grilling and toss 2 to 3 oak wood chunks onto hot coals for smoking; If you are using a wireless meat thermometer, insert one of its probe in the deepest section of the prime rib without touching the bones; Cook until the internal temperature of the roast reaches between 120°F to 130°F depending on desired doneness;

4 Remove the roast from the grill and place into an aluminum drip pan; Cover with foil and let rest for 30 minutes; Slice and serve.

COWBOY PORTERHOUSE
& HICKORY BROWN SUGAR BEANS

Steak

porterhouse steak,
2 inches thick

Steak Seasonings

2 Tbsp black peppercorns

2 Tbsp coarse salt

½ Tbsp dried onions

½ Tbsp red pepper flakes

½ Tbsp dried garlic

Hickory Brown Sugar Beans

15 oz white beans

15 oz pinto beans

¾ cup bacon, chopped

1 cup onions, chopped

1 cup ketchup

1 cup brown sugar

1 Tbsp apple cider vinegar

1 Tbsp worcestershire sauce

1 Tbsp dijon mustard

1 tsp steak seasoning

Additional Equipment

hickory wood chunks for smoking

COWBOY PORTERHOUSE & HICKORY BROWN SUGAR BEANS

Recommended for	Cooking time	Serves
Charcoal or gas grill	45 min to 1 h	1 to 3

1 Preheat your grill for a two-zone cooking — having hot coals on one side and nothing on the other; If you are using a gas grill, turn half the burners to high and leave the other half closed;

2 Dump all Steak Seasonings ingredients into an empty pepper mill and shake; Generously grind about 1 Tbsp of steak seasoning on each side of the porterhouse steak then let rest for 45 min at room temperature;

3 Place a cast iron skillet over high heat and mix all Hickory Brown Sugar Beans ingredients except the beans; Simmer for 5 minutes then add the beans and move the skillet to indirect; Add hickory wood chunks onto hot coals, close the lid and cook for 30 minutes;

4 Grill the porterhouse steak over direct heat for 4 to 6 minutes per side or until desired doneness; It is recommended to close the lid to reduce flare-ups and prevent the steak from burning on its surface;

5 Let the steak rest for 10 minutes and serve.

STEAK SEASONING

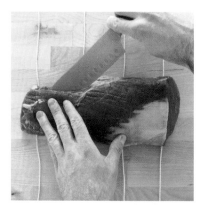

TENDERLOIN CHEESESTEAK

Recommended for	Cooking time	Serves
Charcoal or gas grill	15 min to 25 min	6

1 Preheat your grill for medium heat;

2 In a preheated skillet, sauté the vegetables with canola oil and balsamic vinegar; Add salt and pepper to taste;

3 Cut the tenderloin lengthwise and open like a book; Place the provolone cheese and grilled vegetables inside; Close and secure with butcher strings; Season the exterior with salt, pepper and garlic powder to taste;

4 Grill over direct heat for 8 to 10 minutes per side or until the internal temperature of the meat reaches between 125°F and 145°F on an instant read thermometer; Remove from the grill and let rest for 5 minutes;

5 Cut into slices of 1¼ thick and serve; This dish goes well with a spicy mayo.

Cheesesteak

2 to 3 pounds center cut beef tenderloin

1 Tbsp canola oil

¼ cup onions, sliced

¼ cup red bell peppers

1 jalapeño, sliced

1 clove garlic, minced

1 ½ Tbsp balsamic vinegar

1 Tbsp salt

1 Tbsp black pepper

1 Tbsp garlic powder

4 slices of provolone cheese

Additional Equipment

butcher string

JAILHOUSE STEAKS

Recommended for
Charcoal or gas grill

Cooking time
8 min to 12 min

Serves
4

This quick and easy recipe shows you how to turn an inexpensive piece of meat into a juicy and delightful steak you'll be proud to serve to all your friends. The recipe earned its name because of its simplicity and the availability of the required ingredients.

1 Mix all the ingredients in a container with the steaks and let marinate for 1 to 2 hours;

2 Preheat your grill for direct grilling;

3 Grill each steaks for about 4 to 6 minutes per side or until desired doneness.

Steaks

4 hanger steaks of about 1¼" thick

6 garlic cloves, crushed

½ cup green onions, chopped

2 Tbsp red pepper flakes

2 Tbsp salt

2 Tbsp ground black pepper

¼ cup worcestershire sauce

¼ cup vegetable oil

8 cup apple juice

3 oz dark rum or bourbon (optional)

COFFEE MUG CHILI

Recommended for
Charcoal or gas grill

Cooking time
1 h to 1 h 30

Serves
6

Watching the sunset from the porch while eating a hot cup of chili has never been so comforting.

1 Preheat your grill for indirect cooking;

2 Combine the ground beef with the worcestershire sauce and ½ Tbsp of ground black pepper; Divide into 4 equal patties and place them on the grill for indirect; Toss a few wood chunks onto hot coals for smoking and close the lid; Cook for 20 minutes at 350°F;

3 In a large container, crush the beef patties until you get 1/2-inch chunks, then add all Chili ingredients and mix;

4 Fill the coffee mugs with chili and place them on the grill grate for indirect cooking; Close the lid and cook for 45 minutes at 350°F; Top each mugs with shredded cheddar cheese and close the lid for another 10 minutes;

5 Using heat resistant BBQ gloves, remove the mugs from the grill and let the them cool down for 15 minutes before serving; Top with your favorite hot sauce (optional).

Beef
2 pounds ground beef
¼ cup worcestershire sauce
½ Tbsp black pepper

Chili
2 cups pinto beans
28 oz diced tomatoes
1 medium onion, diced
1 jalapeño, partially seeded and diced
1 garlic clove, minced
2 Tbsp chili powder
1 tsp cumin
2 tsp oregano
1 Tbsp bbq seasonings
¼ cup ketchup
¾ cup black coffee
¼ cup beer
1 Tbsp lime juice

For topping
1 cup old cheddar cheese, shredded
your favorite hot sauce (optional)

Additional Equipment
6 coffee mugs
wood chunks for smoking, preferably hickory
heat resistant bbq gloves

BEEF & STOUT STEW

Stew

2 lb beef sirloin roast
½ cup butter
1 ½ Tbsp flour
1 onion, sliced
2 carrots, diced
1 russet potato, diced
½ turnip, diced
1 cup mushrooms, sliced
¼ cup pitted prunes
1 garlic clove, minced
½ Tbsp salt
1 ½ Tbsp worcestershire sauce
1 can tomato paste
1 cup beef broth
1 large can of stout beer
2 thyme leaves
1 bay leaf
½ Tbsp black pepper

BEEF & STOUT STEW

Recommended for	Cooking time	Serves
Charcoal or gas grill	2 h 30	4

This recipe calls for caveman-style grilling. By cooking the roast directly on the embers, you'll achieve unprecedented barbecue flavors that you simply wouldn't get using a grill grate. Once combined with some roasted barley notes from the stout beer, you will get the perfect dish for a winter's eve.

1 Pour a chimney of hot coals to cover one third of your grill's cooking area; Once the coals are all lit evenly, place the beef sirloin roast directly on the embers and cook for 3 to 4 minutes per side; This method have often been referred to "Caveman Grilling"; It's a very unique way of achieving uncomparable charcoal and smoke aromas with thick pieces of meat;

2 Using barbecue tongs, remove the roast from the fire and brush off any loose ashes that could have stuck to the roast; Slice the roast into cubes of about 2 inches thick;

3 In a preheated cast iron dutch oven, mix ½ cup of melted butter with the sirloin beef cubes and the flour; Add all remaining ingredients to the pot and give a good mix; Cook in indirect for 2h to 2h30 at 350°F.

STEAKHOUSE BEANS

Recommended for	Cooking time	Serves
Smoker	1 h 45 to 2 h	4

1 Preheat your smoker at 250°F;

2 Add the bacon to a preheated cast iron skillet and cook halfway; Add the onions and sliced sirloin steak and continue to cook for a few more minutes; Turn off the heat and mix in all remaining ingredients;

3 Place the skillet in your smoker, toss 3 to 4 wood chunks onto hot coals for smoking and cook for 1h30 to 1h45.

Beans

8 oz sirloin steak, sliced into ¼ thick stripes

6 slices of thick bacon, sliced

¼ cup onions, diced

1 cup pinto beans

1 cup red kidney beans

1 cup black beans

BBQ Sauce

2 Tbsp Kentucky straight bourbon

¼ cup brown sugar

½ cup ketchup

¼ cup molasses

1 ½ Tbsp dijon mustard

3 Tbsp steak sauce

¼ cup apple cider vinegar

2 Tbsp worcestershire sauce

1 Tbsp onion powder

½ Tbsp steak seasoning

¼ cup dark beer

½ tsp liquid smoke

Additional Equipment

wood chunks for smoking, preferably hickory

LEMON PEPPER RIBS

Ribs

2 racks of baby back ribs

3 Tbsp yellow mustard

Lemon Pepper Rub

1 Tbsp lemon coarse sea salt

1 Tbsp freshly ground black pepper

1 tsp paprika

½ Tbsp dried thyme

½ Tbsp minced onions

½ Tbsp minced garlic

1 tsp cayenne pepper flakes

1 tsp brown sugar

1 tsp mace

Lemon Pepper BBQ Sauce

1 Tbsp canola oil

2 garlic cloves, minced

13 oz tomato sauce

1 cup apple cider vinegar

⅔ cup molasses

¼ cup honey

1 Tbsp worcestershire sauce

1 Tbsp dijon mustard

½ tsp liquid smoke

1 tsp onion powder

1 Tbsp freshly ground black pepper

zest and juice from 1 lemon

Additional Equipment

½ cup hickory or oak wood chips

aluminum foil pan

LEMON PEPPER RIBS

Recommended for	Cooking time	Serves
Charcoal grill	2 h to 3 h	2 to 4

1 Preheat your grill for indirect cooking; Place an aluminum drip pan filled with water under the grate and pour a chimney of hot coals alongside to separate the two cooking zones;

2 Mix all Lemon Pepper Rub ingredients in a bowl and set aside;

3 Using a butter knife and a folded paper towel, remove the membrane under each rack of ribs by inserting the knife between the membrane and one of the bones, use the paper towel to get a better grip on the membrane and remove it completely; Brush the ribs with yellow mustard and season both sides with the lemon pepper rub;

4 Place the ribs on the grill for indirect cooking and toss a handful of wood chips onto hot coals for smoking; Cook for 1h30 to 2h at about 350°F.

5 Prepare the Lemon Pepper BBQ Sauce while the ribs are cooking; First, sauté the garlic in canola oil until golden brown then add all remaining ingredients and simmer for 20 minutes;

6 You know that the ribs are done when the meat has shrunk of about 1 inch from the bones; Glaze the ribs with Lemon Pepper BBQ Sauce and sear over high heat for 1 minutes per side.

CLASSIC HICKORY
SMOKED RIBS

Ribs

4 portions of baby back ribs
1 Tbsp dijon mustard

Rub

3 Tbsp brown sugar
3 Tbsp smoked paprika
1 Tbsp ground black pepper
2 tsp salt
1 tsp onion powder

Mop Sauce

3 cup cider vinegar
1 cup olive oil
1 chopped onion
1 Tbsp red pepper flakes
1 Tbsp hot sauce
½ Tbsp salt
½ Tbsp pepper

BBQ Sauce

3 cup ketchup
¾ cup apple cider vinegar
¾ cup water
3 Tbsp worcestershire sauce
¾ cup brown sugar
2 Tbsp molasses
1 Tbsp chili powder
2 tsp onion powder
2 tsp cumin
2 Tbsp paprika
2 tsp garlic powder
1 tsp yellow mustard
1 tsp lemon juice
1 tsp salt
1 tsp ground black pepper

Additional Equipment

hickory wood chunks for smoking
basting mop

CLASSIC HICKORY SMOKED RIBS

Recommended for	Cooking time	Serves
Smoker	4 h	4 to 6

1 Preheat your smoker at 275°F;

2 Using a butter knife and a folded paper towel, remove the thick skin membrane under the ribs; Baste the ribs with dijon mustard;

3 In a bowl, mix the brown sugar, smoked paprika, onion powder, black pepper and salt, then season ribs on both side;

4 Place ribs in your smoker with a few hickory wood chunks onto hot coals for smoking; Cook for 4h to 5h at between 250°F to 275°F;

5 Mop the ribs every hours — see mop sauce preparation below;

6 You know the ribs are done when the meat shrunk about one inch from the bones; Glaze the ribs with BBQ Sauce 15 minutes before removing from the smoker.

MOP SAUCE

1 Mix the cider vinegar, olive oil, chopped onions, red pepper flakes, hot sauce, salt and pepper in a saucepan;

2 Bring to a simmer for 15 minutes.

BBQ SAUCE

1 Mix the ketchup, brown sugar, molasses, chili powder, onion powder, cumin, paprika, garlic powder, worcestershire sauce, apple cider vinegar, yellow mustard, lemon juice, water, salt and pepper in a saucepan;

2 Bring to a simmer for 20 minutes.

MAPLE CAYENNE RIBS

Recommended for
Charcoal or gas grill

Cooking time
4 h to 4 h 30

Serves
2 to 4

Slowly smoked using maple wood, these sweet and spicy baby back ribs make a luxurious addition to any menu. Serve with thick-cut fries and enjoy.

1 Preheat your grill for indirect: Place an aluminum foil pan filled with water under the grill grate and toss a chimney of hot coals alongside;

2 With a butter knife and some paper towels, remove the membrane under each slab of ribs by inserting the knife between the membrane and one of the bone, pull the membrane with the paper towel to remove it completely;

3 Mix all Rub ingredients and apply the rub on both side of the ribs with your hands so it penetrates the meat;

4 Place the ribs on the grill grate over indirect heat and toss a cup of wood chips onto hot coals for smoking; Close the lid and cook for about 4 hours at 250°F;

5 Mix all Glaze ingredients in a saucepan and simmer for 15 minutes; Glaze the ribs 10 to 15 minutes before removing them from the grill; The ribs are done when the meat has shrunk about 1 inch from the bones;

6 Cover the ribs with aluminum foil and let them rest for 15 minutes before serving.

Ribs
2 slabs of baby back ribs

Rub
¼ cup brown sugar
½ Tbsp salt
2 Tbsp ground coriander
1 tsp cinnamon
1 tsp ground cumin
2 tsp black pepper

Glaze
½ cup maple syrup
¼ cup cayenne hot sauce
¼ cup butter
¼ cup ketchup
1 tsp lime zest
2 Tbsp lime juice

Additional Equipment
1 cup wood chips, preferably maple

Pork

8 to 10 pound Boston butt
(pork shoulder)

2 cups apple cider vinegar

coleslaw (optional)

burger buns

Sweet and spicy rub

2 Tbsp paprika

2 Tbsp brown sugar

2 Tbsp sugar

1 Tbsp salt

½ Tbsp garlic powder

½ Tbsp black pepper

1 tsp cayenne powder

Honey Cayenne BBQ Sauce

2 Tbsp butter

1 white onion, sliced

1 Tbsp sweet and spicy rub

1 cup ketchup

½ cup cayenne hot sauce

1 cup honey

2 Tbsp cayenne pepper flakes

1 ¾ cup apple cider vinegar

Additional Equipment

wood chunks for smoking, preferably a blend of apple and oak

HONEY CAYENNE PULLED PORK

Recommended for	Cooking time	Serves
Smoker	8 h to 10 h	6 to 10

1 Preheat your smoker at 250°F;

2 Mix all Rub ingredients in a bowl and generously season the pork shoulder on all sides;

3 Place the pork shoulder in your smoker and toss about 1 lb of wood chunks onto hot coals (preferably oak and apple) for smoking; Cook until the internal temperature of the shoulder reach 205°F — this should take between 8 to 10 hours if you keep your smoker at 250°F; Keep the meat moist by spraying, basting or mopping with apple cider vinegar every hour from mid cooking up to the end;

4 In a preheated sauce pan, sauté the onions with 2 Tbsp of butter until golden brown then add all remaining Honey Cayenne BBQ Sauce ingredients and simmer for 15 minutes;

5 Once the pork butt has reached an internal temperature of 205°F on an instant read thermometer, remove from the smoker and cover with aluminum foil for about 1 hour;

6 Shred the pork with your hands using thick heat resistant rubber gloves or a pair of meat claws; Assemble the sandwiches in grilled burger buns with Honey Cayenne BBQ Sauce and coleslaw (optional).

CAROLINA-STYLE PULLED PORK

Recommended for
Smoker

Cooking time
7 h to 10 h

Serves
8 to 12

1 Preheat your smoker at around 225°F;

2 Mix all Rub ingredients and apply a generous coating on each side of the pork shoulder;

3 Place the pork shoulder in your smoker and toss 5 to 6 wood chunks onto hot coals for smoking; Cook until the internal temperature of the meat reaches 205°F; Cooking time is about 7 to 10 hours – it is recommended to use a wireless meat thermometer inserted into the deepest section of the meat so you don't have to constantly take the temperature of the meat near the end of the cooking time;

4 Spray the shoulder with apple cider vinegar every hour during cooking to keep it from dehydrating;

5 In a saucepan, mix the Finishing Sauce ingredients and bring to a simmer for 5 minutes;

6 Once the pork should have reached an internal temperature of 205°F, remove from the smoker and let rest for 1 hour at room temperature;

7 Using heat resistant kitchen gloves or meat claws, shred the pork shoulder and discard all bones and big chunks of fat; Add in the Finishing Sauce, barbecue seasonings and barbecue sauce;

8 Assemble in burger buns with coleslaw (optional).

Pork
6 to 10 pounds pork shoulder
2 cup apple cider vinegar
2 Tbsp barbecue seasonings
2 cup barbecue sauce
coleslaw (optional)
burger buns

Rub
2 Tbsp paprika
2 Tbsp brown sugar
1 Tbsp onion powder
1 Tbsp chili powder
2 tsp garlic salt
2 tsp celery salt
1 tsp black pepper
1 tsp white pepper
1 tsp cumin

Finishing Sauce
2 cup apple cider vinegar
1 cup water
¼ cup brown sugar
1 Tbsp salt
1 Tbsp red pepper flakes
2 tsp black pepper
2 tsp hot sauce

Additional Equipment
grilling & smoking meat thermometer
aluminum drip pan
wood chunks for smoking, preferably apple, oak and/ or cherry

OKTOBERFEST SKILLET

Recommended for
Charcoal or gas grill

Cooking time
1 h to 1 h 30

Serves
2 to 4

This recipe has taken a seasonal favorite and given it a fabulous culinary twist. This meaty dish has all the spices and herbs you could possibly want for an autumn night but it is the texture that really brings the meal to life. Crunchy bacon, crispy potatoes, and beer-soaked bratwurst all bursting with warmth will liven up the party. Serve with German beer and pretzels for the ultimate Oktoberfest experience.

1 Preheat your grill for a two-zone cooking — having hot coals on one side and nothing on the other; If you are using a gas grill, turn half the burners to high and leave the other half closed;

2 Combine the diced potatoes, olive oil and caraway seeds in a cast iron skillet and cook in indirect for 30 to 45 minutes or until the potatoes are done;

3 Grill the bacon and brats over direct heat for about 3 minutes per side; Slice into 1 inch chunks and combine with all the remaining ingredients in the skillet;

4 Cook in indirect for another 20 minutes and serve.

Skillet
- 2 white potatoes
- 2 Tbsp olive oil
- ½ Tbsp caraway seeds
- 4 thick bacon slices
- 4 german brats
- 1 medium yellow onion, diced
- 1 red apple, diced
- ⅓ red cabbage, diced
- 1 Tbsp dijon mustard
- ½ cup sauerkraut
- 12 oz German style beer
- 1 tsp freshly ground black pepper
- ½ tsp ground nutmeg

THE FATTY

Recommended for
Smoker

Cooking time
2 h

Serves
4 to 6

Carefully arranged bacon encasing rich sausage meat, jalapeños and cheese. This feast will definitely be the center of attention.

1 Preheat your smoker between 275°F and 300°F;

2 Make a bacon weave using all 14 slices;

3 In a bowl, mix all Dry Rub ingredients then sprinkle 1 Tbsp over the bacon weave;

4 Combine the pork sausage meat and ground beef; Layer the meat over the bacon weave like a blanket then add the cheddar cheese, jalapeños, red onions and green onions;

5 Roll the fatty into a log then season the exterior with more BBQ rub;

6 Place the Fatty in your smoker and toss 4 to 5 wood chunks onto hot coals for smoking; Cook for 2 hours or until the internal temperature of the meat reads 160°F on an instant read thermometer; Brush with BBQ sauce for the last hour of cooking.

7 Remove from smoker and let rest for 15 minutes before slicing and serving.

Fatty
1 pound bacon (approx. 14 slices)
1 pound pork sausage meat
½ pound ground beef
1 cup shredded cheddar cheese
4 jalapeños, diced
1 red onion, diced
¼ cup green onions, sliced
¼ cup bbq sauce

Dry Rub
1 Tbsp paprika
1 Tbsp brown sugar
½ Tbsp ground black pepper
½ Tbsp salt
½ tsp cumin

Additional Equipment
wood chunks for smoking, preferably hickory and/or oak

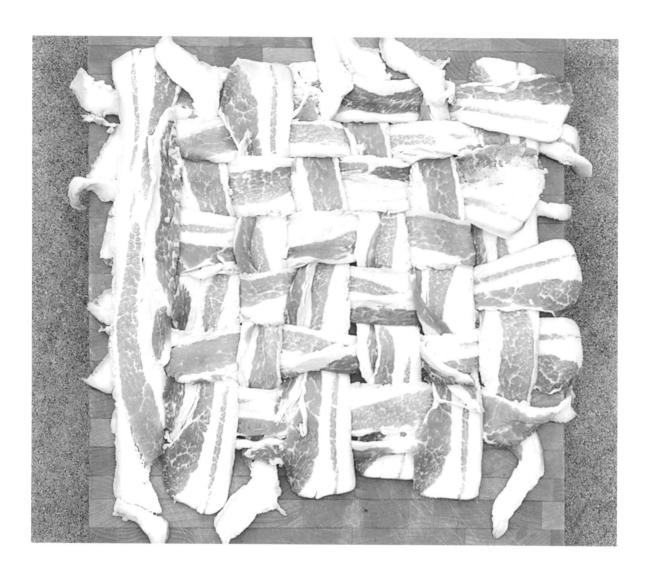

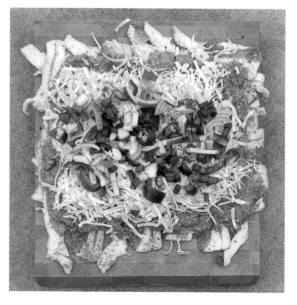

Pulled Chicken

1 to 2 whole chickens

coleslaw

burger buns

mayonnaise or your favorite condiment

Carolina Style BBQ Rub

½ Tbsp paprika

1 tsp garlic powder

1 Tbsp salt

½ Tbsp ground white pepper

½ Tbsp ground black pepper

½ Tbsp brown sugar

1 tsp mustard

½ tsp cumin

Bacon & Bourbon BBQ Sauce

½ cup bacon, sliced

⅓ cup onions, diced

⅓ cup bourbon

⅔ cup brown sugar

1 cup apple cider vinegar

1 cup ketchup

1 tsp red pepper flakes

½ Tbsp salt

1 tsp ground black pepper

Additional Equipment

aluminum drip pans

wood chunks for smoking, preferably apple & hickory

BACON BOURBON PULLED CHICKEN

Recommended for	Cooking time	Serves
Smoker	1 h 30 to 2 h	4 to 6

1 Preheat your smoker between 225°F and 250°F;

2 Using kitchen shears or a sharp knife, remove the chicken's backbone and make a cut through the breastbone from the inside so the chicken can lay flat like an open book;

3 Combine all Carolina Style BBQ Rub ingredients and season the chicken on both sides;

4 Place the chicken in your smoker and toss 3 to 4 wood chunks onto hot coals for smoking; Cook until the internal temperature of the meat reads 165°F on an instant read thermometer;

5 In a saucepan, cook the bacon and the onions until golden brown then add all remaining Bacon & Bourbon BBQ Sauce ingredients; Simmer for 10 minutes;

6 Once the bird has reached an internal temperature of 165°F, remove from the smoker and let rest at room temperature 20 minutes;

7 Using heat resistant kitchen gloves or meat claws, shred the chicken and discard the bones; Add in 2 cups of Bacon & Bourbon BBQ Sauce per shredded chicken;

8 Assemble the sandwiches in grilled burger buns with mayonnaise, pulled chicken and coleslaw.

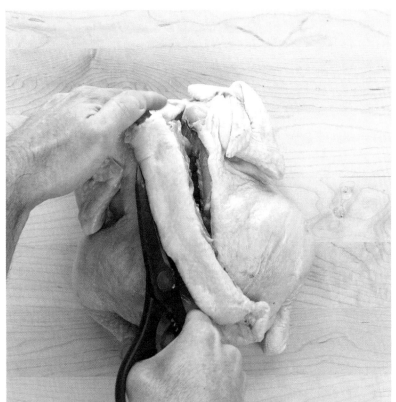

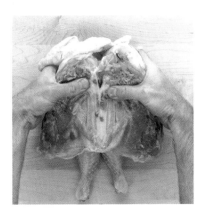

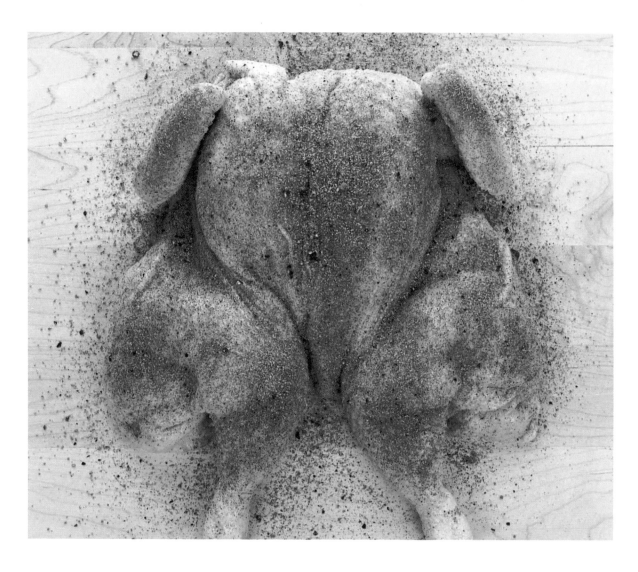

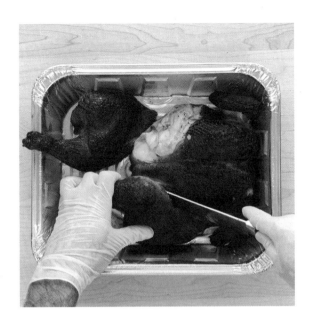

CHICKEN UNDER A BRICK

CHICKEN UNDER A BRICK

Recommended for	**Cooking time**	**Serves**
Charcoal grill	30 min to 40 min	2 to 4

This Portuguese-style chicken is easy to make and packs real flavor. Placing some bricks on top of the chicken allows you to fully grill the bird over direct heat without burning the skin. Chargrill some garlic bread and serve with a fresh tomato bruschetta.

1 Using kitchen shears or a sharp knife, remove the chicken's backbone and make a cut through the breastbone from the inside so the chicken can lay flat like an open book;

2 In a bowl, combine all Wet Rub ingredients then apply on both sides of the chicken; Cover and let marinate for 1 hour in the refrigerator;

3 Preheat your grill for direct grilling over medium heat;

4 Lay the chicken skin side down on the hot grate and place the two bricks on top; Grill for 10 to 15 minutes with the lid closed then flip the chicken and put place back the bricks; Cook for another 15 minutes with the lid closed or until the internal temperature of the meat reads 165°F on an instant read thermometer;

5 Place the lemon directly onto hot coals and char it for 1 to 2 minutes per side;

6 Once the chicken is done, remove from the grill and pour some lemon juice on top; Let rest for 10 minutes and serve.

Chicken
1 whole chicken

1 lemon

grilled garlic bread (optional)

Wet Rub
2 Tbsp freshly chopped thyme

1 Tbsp grated lemon zest

4 garlic cloves, minced

1 Tbsp coarse sea salt

1 Tbsp freshly ground black pepper

2 Tbsp olive oil

Additional Equipment
1 or 2 bricks wrapped in aluminum foil

TEQUILA LEMON CHICKEN

Recommended for
Charcoal grill

Cooking time
45 min to 1 h 15

Serves
2 to 4

1 Combine all Tequila Lemon Marinade ingredients and pour over the two chicken halves; Cover and let marinade for 2 hours in the refrigerator;

2 Preheat your grill for a two-zone cooking — having hot coals on one side and nothing on the other; If you are using a gas grill, turn half the burners to high and leave the other half closed;

3 Place the chicken in your grill for indirect cooking and toss a few wood chunks onto hot coals for smoking; Close the lid and cook for 1 hour at 400°F or until the internal temperature of the meat reads 165°F on an instant read thermometer;

4 Grill the chicken halves over direct heat for 2 minutes per side; Remove from the grill and let rest for 10 minutes before serving.

Chicken
1 whole chicken, splitted into halves

Tequila Lemon Marinade
2 Tbsp olive oil

2 Tbsp tequila

2 Tbsp paprika

1 Tbsp coarse sea salt

2 Tbsp dried rosemary

1 Tbsp cayenne pepper flakes

3 minced garlic cloves

1 Tbsp freshly ground black pepper

juice from half a lemon

Additional Equipment
wood chunks for smoking, preferably tequila wood barrel chunks but can be substituted for oak wood chunks

CHIPOTLE BEER CAN CHICKEN

Recommended for
Charcoal or gas grill

Cooking time
1 h to 1 h 30

Serves
2 to 4

1 Preheat your grill for indirect cooking;

2 Rinse the chicken then pat dry with paper towels; Brush the bird with olive oil;

3 Combine all Rub ingredients in a bowl and mix with your fingers to break any lumps; Season the chicken on all sides with the rub;

4 Pour half the beer onto the wood chips then insert the can in the chicken's cavity and make the bird stand breast side up; Place the bird on the grill for indirect cooking and toss the beer soaked wood chips onto hot coals for smoking; Close the lid and cook for 45 to 90 minutes or until the internal temperature of the meat reads 165°F on an instant read thermometer;

5 In a cast iron skillet or sauce pan, saute the onions and garlic with olive oil then add all the remaining Chipotle BBQ Sauce ingredients and simmer for 10 minutes;

6 Brush the chicken with chipotle bbq sauce for the last 10 minutes; Once the chicken in fully cooked, remove from the grill and let rest for 10 minutes before serving.

Chicken
1 whole chicken
1 Tbsp olive oil
1 can of your favorite beer

Rub
½ Tbsp paprika
½ Tbsp brown sugar
1 tsp chipotle powder
1 tsp salt
1 tsp black pepper

Chipotle BBQ Sauce
1 Tbsp olive oil
¼ cup onions, minced
1 garlic clove, minced
2 chipotle chiles in adobo, chopped
1 cup ketchup
⅓ cup brown sugar
¼ cup apple cider vinegar
1 Tbsp worcestershire sauce
½ Tbsp dijon mustard
½ Tbsp lime juice
1 tsp salt
1 tsp ground black pepper

Additional Equipment
1 cup of wood chips for smoking, preferably hickory

SMOKED TURKEY LEGS WITH HABANERO MANGO SAUCE

Recommended for
Smoker

Cooking time
1 h to 1 h 30

Serves
2 to 4

1 Preheat your smoker at 250°F;

2 In a bowl, combine all Dry Rub ingredients; Brush the turkey legs with olive oil then season both sides with the rub;

3 Place the turkey legs in your smoker and toff a few wood chunks onto hot coals for smoking; Cook for 1h to 1h30 or until the interior of the meat reaches 165°F on an instant read thermometer;

4 In a saucepan, combine all Habanero Mango BBQ Sauce ingredients and simmer for 20 minutes;

5 Brush the turkey legs with Habanero Mango BBQ Sauce on the last 15 minutes.

Turkey Legs
4 turkey legs
2 Tbsp olive oil

Dry Rub
2 tsp paprika
1 tsp dried thyme
1 tsp dried oregano
2 tsp garlic powder
1 tsp onion powder
1 tsp salt
1 tsp black pepper

Habanero Mango BBQ Sauce
1 cup ketchup
1 cup mango juice
1 ½ Tbsp habanero hot sauce
¼ cup worcestershire sauce
2 Tbsp steak sauce
1 tsp onion powder
½ tsp black pepper

Additional Equipment
wood chunks for smoking, preferably apple or cherry

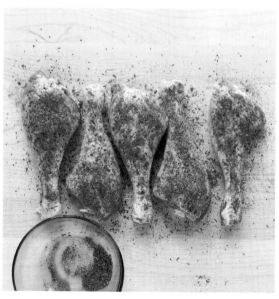

CHRISTMAS FATTY

Recommended for
Smoker

Cooking time
2 h

Serves
4 to 6

Smoked using cherry and apple wood chunks then glazed with barbeque sauce to caramelize the outer edge. This christmas variation of the so-called "Fatty" will enhance any seasonal menu.

1 Preheat your smoker between 275°F and 300°F;

2 Make a bacon weave using all 14 slices;

3 Combine the ground turkey and pork sausage meat; Layer the meat over the bacon weave like a blanket then add the shredded cheddar cheese, asparagus, brie cheese, dried cranberries and red onions;

4 Roll into a log and season with cajun seasonings or your favorite bbq rub;

5 Place the fatty in your smoker and toss 4 to 5 wood chunks onto hot coals for smoking; Cook for 2 hours or until the internal temperature of the meat reaches 165°F on an instant read thermometer; Brush with BBQ sauce for the last hour of cooking;

6 Remove from smoker and let rest for 15 minutes before slicing and serving.

Fatty
14 slices of bacon
1 lb ground turkey
½ lb pork sausage meat
2 cup shredded cheddar cheese
4 slices of brie cheese
4 asparagus
¼ cup dried cranberries
¼ cup red onions, chopped
1 Tbsp cajun seasoning
2 Tbsp bbq sauce

Additional Equipment
wood chunks for smoking, preferably cherry or apple

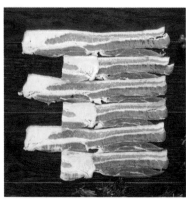

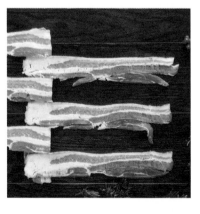

FIRE ROASTED SEAFOOD

MANGO FISH TACOS

Recommended for	Cooking time	Serves
Charcoal or gas grill	6 min to 10 min	4

Deliciously seasoned grilled white fish, flaked into warm flour tacos and topped with a sweet mango salsa makes a quick and easy meal that harmonizes well with the hottest days of summer. Get yourself a cold cerveza and enjoy the quality time.

1 Preheat your grill at medium-high for direct grilling;

2 Combine all Sriracha Mayo ingredients and set aside in the refrigerator;

3 In a bowl, gently mix all Mango Salsa ingredients and set aside for later;

4 Brush the fillets with olive oil then add the lime juice and Tex-Mex seasonings;

5 Place the fish fillets in a preheated and highly seasoned cast iron skillet and place the skillet on the grill over direct heat; Close the lid and cook for 3 minutes, then flip the fish and cook for another 3 minutes;

6 Grill each tortillas for 10 sec per sides;

7 Assemble the tacos with grilled fish, salsa, spicy mayo and some chopped cilantro on top (optional).

Tacos
4 whitefish fillets
¼ cup olive oil
2 Tbsp lime juice
1 Tbsp Tex-Mex seasoning
flour tortillas
2 Tbsp fresh cilantro, chopped (optional)

Mango Salsa
1 cup mangoes, diced
½ cup red bell peppers, diced
½ cup cucumbers, diced
⅓ cup red onions, diced
1 Tbsp fresh mint, chopped
1 Tbsp lime juice
2 Tbsp olive oil

Sriracha Mayo
1 cup mayonnaise
1 Tbsp sriracha
½ tsp lime juice

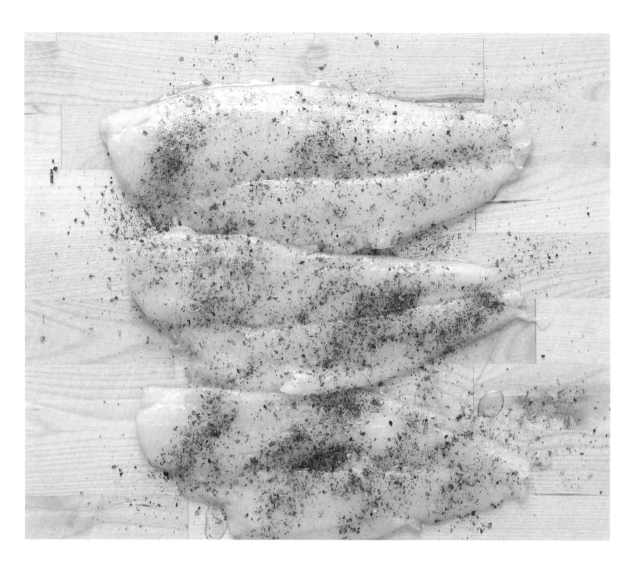

TIPSY SHRIMP

Recommended for
Charcoal or gas grill

Cooking time
20 min

Serves
3 to 4

Forget the usual mop sauce, this recipe calls for a cocktail shaker sauce! Chargrilled to perfection, these jumbo shrimp receive the full treatment: flambéed with a spiced rum and lime juice blend then brushed with a buttery coconut glaze. These tipsy shrimp are just what you need to kickstart any outdoor gathering.

1 Preheat your grill for direct grilling over medium heat (about 350°F);

2 Thread 3 to 4 shrimp onto each skewer and season with coarse sea salt and freshly ground black pepper;

3 Combine all Shaker Sauce ingredients in a cocktail shaker (or in any other type of container) and mix;

4 In a saucepan, combine the butter and cornstarch and mix over medium heat; Add all Coconut Rum Glaze ingredients and simmer for 10 minutes;

5 Grill the shrimp over direct heat for about 3 to 4 minutes per sides; Pour some shaker sauce over the cooking shrimps every minutes or so (be careful for the flames);

6 Brush the shrimp with the coconut rum glaze on the last minute; Keep the remaining glaze for a dipping sauce.

Shrimps
20 jumbo shrimp
½ Tbsp coarse sea salt
½ Tbsp freshly ground black pepper
½ Tbsp grated coconut (optional)

Shaker Sauce
¼ cup spiced rum
2 Tbsp brown sugar
1 tsp garlic salt
2 Tbsp white vinegar
2 Tbsp coconut oil
juice from half a lime

Coconut Rum Glaze
¼ lb unsalted butter, melted
½ Tbsp cornstarch
½ cup brown sugar
1 Tbsp honey
⅓ cup heavy cream
⅓ cup unsweetened coconut milk
½ cup spiced rum
1 tsp orange zest
1 egg yolk
juice from half an orange

Additional Equipment
skewers

TUNA STEAKS WITH JALAPENO PEACH SALSA

Recommended for
Charcoal or gas grill

Cooking time
6 min to 10 min

Serves
4

Grilled over a raging hot charcoal fire, these 2-inch thick tuna steaks might just replace T-Bones at your next get together. Pair them with a fresh jalapeño and peach salsa and you are all set for a memorable dinner.

1 Preheat your grill at high temperature;

2 Combine all Rub ingredients in a bowl or in a dry rub shaker; Brush the tuna steaks on both sides with sesame oil and season with the rub;

3 In a bowl, combine all Jalapeño Peach Salsa ingredients and gently mix;

4 Grill the steaks over high heat for 3 minutes per side;

5 Cut the tuna steaks into ¼ thick slices and serve with the jalapeño peach salsa on the side.

Steaks
4 tuna steaks of about
2 inches thick
2 Tbsp sesame oil

Rub
½ Tbsp bay leaf powder
½ Tbsp celery salt
½ Tbsp smoked paprika
½ Tbsp dry mustard
¼ tsp cayenne powder
¼ tsp ground mace
¼ tsp ground cardamon

Jalapeño Peach Salsa
1 cup diced peaches
½ cup diced jalapeños
½ cup diced cucumbers
½ cup diced red onions
1 Tbsp lime juice
2 Tbsp brown sugar
½ tsp ginger
½ cup cilantro
½ tsp salt
1 Tbsp olive oil

HOT SMOKED SCALLOPS

Recommended for
Charcoal grill

Cooking time
20 min to 30 min

Serves
4 as an appetizer

Alder smoke flavors combined with cajun seasonings and a rich and creamy lemon butter sauce. Serve these scallops steaming hot on a cast iron plate with a couple sprigs of dill.

1 Preheat your grill for indirect;

2 Combine all Seasoning ingredients in a bowl and season the scallops on all sides;

3 Place the scallops in your grill for indirect and toss 1 cup of wood chips onto hot coals for smoking; Close the lid and cook for 20 to 30 minutes or until desired doneness;

4 Melt the butter in a skillet or saucepan then whisk in the white wine, heavy cream, lemon juice and minced garlic; Simmer for 15 minutes then transfer ¾ to a dipping bowl and use the remaining to brush the scallops during the last 5 minutes of cooking;

5 Remove the scallops from the grill and serve; Sprinkle some seasonings over the lemon butter sauce and add 2 sprigs of fresh dill on top.

Scallops
2 pounds jumbo sized scallops (8 to 12 per pound)

Seasoning
½ Tbsp salt
½ Tbsp paprika
½ Tbsp oregano
1 tsp cayenne powder
1 tsp chili powder
1 tsp white pepper
1 tsp black pepper
1 tsp onion powder
1 tsp garlic powder
½ tsp cumin

Lemon Butter Sauce
½ stick butter
3 Tbsp white wine
2 Tbsp heavy cream
the juice from half a lemon
1 garlic clove, minced
2 sprigs of fresh dill
½ tsp seasoning

Additional Equipment
1 cup wood chips for smoking, preferably alder

PESTO
SALMON
DARNES

Darnes

2 salmon darnes, 1½ to
2 inches thick

1 Tbsp coarse sea salt

½ Tbsp freshly ground
black pepper

Pesto

2 cup fresh basil leaves

3 Tbsp olive oil

2 ½ Tbsp pine nuts

2 cloves garlic

PESTO SALMON DARNES

Recommended for	Cooking time	Serves
Charcoal or gas grill	15 min	2

Gentle aromatic notes from the basil combined with a crunchy burst of garlicky and salty flavor will have you rethink the way you used to prepare salmon.

1 Preheat your grill at medium/high temperature;

2 Combine all Pesto ingredients in a food processor and blend until smooth;

3 Season the salmon darnes with coarse sea salt and freshly ground black pepper then apply a generous coating of pesto on both sides;

4 Grill the darnes for 3 to 4 minutes per side over direct heat; Serve.

DESSERTS
FROM THE GRILL

S'MORES BANANA BOATS

Recommended for
Charcoal or gas grill

Cooking time
6 min to 8 min

Serves
4

Boats
4 bananas
⅔ cup chocolate chips
1 cup miniature marshmallows
4 graham crackers, crushed

Additional Equipment
stainless steel taco holder or aluminum foil

1 Preheat your grill for indirect cooking at 350°F;

2 Combine the chocolate chips, mini marshmallows and crushed graham crackers in a bowl;

3 Cut an opening lengthwise in each banana and stuff the s'mores mix inside;

4 Place each stuffed bananas on a taco rack (if you don't have a taco rack you can crumple some aluminum foil around each banana to hold them in place) and cook in indirect for 6 to 8 minutes.

BLUEBERRY CRUMBLE

Recommended for
Charcoal grill

Cooking time
30 min

Serves
4 to 6

Give a twist to any crumble by cooking them on the grill with some apple wood chips for a gentle smokey addition.

1 Preheat your grill for indirect cooking;

2 Combine the blueberries, lemon zest and cane sugar in a cast iron skillet;

3 In a bowl, combine the brown sugar, flour, oatmeal, cinnamon and coconut oil; Layer the crumble over the blueberries;

4 Place the skillet over indirect and toss a handful of wood chip onto hot coals for smoking; Close the lid and cook for 30 minutes; Serve with vanilla ice cream.

Blueberry Crumble
5 cup blueberries
2 Tbsp cane sugar
1 tsp lemon zest
vanilla ice cream
½ cup brown sugar
½ cup flour
¾ cup oatmeal
1 tsp cinnamon
½ cup coconut oil

Additional Equipment
½ cup apple wood chips for smoking

STRAWBERRY BROCHETTES

Recommended for
Charcoal or gas grill

Cooking time
8 min

Serves
2

1 Preheat your grill for medium/high;

2 In a bowl, gently mix the strawberries, triple sec, vanilla extract and sugar; Thread onto skewers with a chunk of sponge cake separating each strawberries;

3 Grill the brochettes over direct heat for 4 to 5 minutes per side;

4 Top with chocolate syrup and serve.

Brochettes
1 pound strawberries, sliced in half
1 pound sponge cake
¾ cup sugar
2 oz triple sec
½ tsp vanilla extract

Topping
chocolate syrup

Additional Equipment
skewers

GRILLED BUTTERSCOTCH PEACHES

Peaches
6 ripe peaches, halves and pitted
½ cup unsalted butter, melted
1 cup cane sugar
½ Tbsp cinnamon
1 tsp ground nutmeg
½ cup crushed pecans
1 cup butterscotch chips
ice cream

Recommended for	Cooking time	Serves
Charcoal or gas grill	8 min	4

1 Preheat your grill at high temperature;

2 Brush the interior of the peaches with melted butter;

3 Combine the cane sugar, cinnamon and ground nutmeg into a bowl; Dip the peaches cut side down into the sugar mix;

4 In a saucepan, slowly heat the butterscotch chips until completely melted;

5 Grill the peaches on both sides for 3 minutes; Remove from the grill and top with ice cream, butterscotch syrup and crushed pecans.

ABOUT GRILLED

In February 2016, our lives took an interesting shift toward the business ventures of barbecuing across social media. Fastforwarding to the present, our clothes now smell like hickory when we get home, we often eat ribs before noon, and we can no longer remember which day of the week it is. That must mean progress, right?

Like a postman on his round, neither snow, nor rain, nor heat, nor gloom of night will keep us from our duty to provide you with ideas and inspiration so you can enjoy some quality time around your grill.

- Kristoffer and Jean-François

INDEX

A

B

C

INDEX

M

Grilled | The Cookbook

Copyright © 2017 by Better Be Grilled Inc.

Published by kchiing publishing | www.kchiing.com

Written by Jean-François Burman & Kristoffer Laurin-Racicot

Photography by Roger Proulx © & Kristoffer Laurin-Racicot ©

Food Styling by Michelle Diamond (p. 30, 34, 38, 62, 120, 168)

With thanks to

Marie-Eve Boivin, for all the help with designs

Pierre-Luc Nantel, for his extreme vibe that keep us pushing further

Simon De l'Est, for his BBQ expertise

Malory Cookware, for the awesome grill grates

Shutterstock credits

Lisovskaya Natalia (p. 2/3)
Arina P Habich (p. 4)
Ramon grosso dolarea (p. 8/9)
Lukas Gojda (p. 46/47)
Artem Shadrin (p. 96/97)
stockcreations (p. 124/125)
stockcreations (p. 147/148)
Elena Shashkina (p. 165/166)

Some of the material in this book may have originally appeared, in different form, on betterbegrilled.com

ISBN 978-90-821336-6-0

Printed in the EU

10 9 8 7 6 5 4 3 2 1

www.betterbegrilled.com

www.facebook.com/betterbegrilled

For media inquiries, corporate & volume sales or any other requests, please contact us at contact@betterbegrilled.com